THE KITCHEN TABLE
Cookbook

written and illustrated by
Lloie Schwartz

Illustrations: Lloie Schwartz

Book Design & photo: Meg Swansen

Logo Design: Elizabeth Zimmermann

Copy Editor: Linda Schultz

© 1996, Schoolhouse Press

ISBN 0-942018-10-9

First Edition, 1996

Printed in the United States of America

For additional copies of this book, contact:
Schoolhouse Press
6899 Cary Bluff
Pittsville, WI 54466
(715) 884-2799

Or, come and have a meal at
The Kitchen Table
118 East Third Street
Marshfield, WI 54449
(715)-387-2601
Serving breakfast & lunch Mon.-Sat. 7am-2pm

Acknowledgements:

Thank you:
To all the known and unknown cooks who have shared their skills and recipes with me. This book does not come from me, it comes through me.

To Meg Swansen, my sister and friend, for the computer graphics and for helping me learn to use her computer, and a whole lot more.

To Linda Schultz, my kitchen manager who did a great job of proof-reading.

To the entire K.T. Crew, especially the "oldies", Linda, Gail, Bonnie and Mary, who made this book possible.

To Stew, who helped create the Kitchen Table Restaurant.

To all my faithful customers who wouldn't stop asking for this book

Preface

From our own secret files, here they are: the actual, un-cut recipes of The Kitchen Table restaurant.

So many of you have asked for them for so long that you finally caused this book to be written. These recipes are only guidelines to arouse your curiosity and stimulate creativity. Make them your own by adding little personal touches. Arranging a piece of music is similar to arranging a recipe. Do your own rendition and let your individual style shine through. Recipes are always evolving. New ideas, new ingredients and new equipment create changes. Think of cooking as an art and express yourself through it. As with any art or skill, the most important thing is a love for it. Once you love to cook, amazing things begin to happen - some good, some not so good!

It's important to realize that you don't <u>have</u> to cook anymore. This is the age of prepared food, so even if you can't cook at all, you can fake it. Therefore, when you do cook, do it with love. When someone prepares their favorite dish, I can taste whether they enjoyed making it. When someone who hates to cook prepares a dish I can taste that too! At The Kitchen Table we cook with joy. We still make all our bread by hand, and that's why it tastes so good. Think about the difference between handmade bread and mechanically made bread; homemade cookies and store-bought cookies; home grown vegetables and commercially grown vegetables; a hand knitted afghan and a machine knitted afghan. See what I mean? Things that are loved into existence have a different energy.

Do what you love and love what you do and your life will be sweeter.

Rosie Schwartz
May 1996

... of Contents

Beautiful Soups - pages 2 - 20

pg. 2 Lou's Mushroom
pg. 3 Potato - Cucumber
pg. 4 Gazpacho with Croutons
pg. 5 Cream of Cauliflower
pg. 6 14 Carrot Gold
pg. 7 Cuban Black Bean
pg. 8 Boston Clam Chowder
pg. 9 Ham & Dumpling
pg. 10 Lentil Vegetable
pg. 11 Garden Pea
pg. 12 Cream of Potato
pg. 13 Cream of Reuben
pg. 14 Cream of Spinach
pg. 15 Tomato Dill
pg. 16 Cream of Turkey & Wild Rice
pg. 17 Cajun Bean
pg. 18 Italian Barley
pg. 19 Chicken or Turkey Dumpling
pg. 20 Russian Borscht

Entrees & Other Stuff - pages 22 - 34

pg. 22 Chicken Normandy
pg. 23 Alaska Crab Sandwich
pg. 24 Creôle Shrimp with Rice
pg. 25 Ratatouille
pg. 26 Stroganoff
pg. 27 Verna's Sandwich
pg. 28 New Orleans Red Beans & Rice
pg. 29 Tørsk
pg. 30 Tamale Torte
pg. 31 Warm Chicken Salad with Orange Rosemary Dressing
pg. 31 Honey Mustard Dressing
pg. 33 Beulah's Salad Dressing
pg. 33 Sauce Moreau
pg. 34 Oma's Bread Stuffing

Cakes & Pies - pages 36 - 54

pg. 36 Cranberry Nut Pie
pg. 37 Granny Smith Apple Pies
pg. 38 Banana Cake
pg. 39 Cheesecake
pg. 40 Carrot Cake
pg. 41 Coffee Cakes
pg. 42 Custard Cups
pg. 43 Cinnamon Rolls
pg. 44 Meggie's Crunchy Granola
pg. 45 Poppy Seed Torte
pg. 46 Pumpkin Pies
pg. 47 Pie Shells
pg. 48 Pumpkin Cake
pg. 49 Strawberry Torte
pg. 50 Swedish Apple Pies
pg. 51 Walnut Pie
pg. 52 French Chocolate Torte
pg. 53 Chocolate Cake
pg. 54 Rhubarb Pies
pg. 55 Index

Lou's Mushroom Soup

- Yield 3 gals. -

5 lbs. mushrooms sliced
3 onions diced
6 qts. water
1 c. beef soup base
1 tsp. pepper
3 bay leaves
1 tsp. ground rosemary
2 cups white wine
4 cups sour cream
roux = 3 c. butter, 3 c. flour

Make roux by cooking butter and flour together in a separate pot for 10 min. Set aside.
Brown onions in some butter. Add mushrooms and sauté until barely cooked.
Add water and seasonings. Bring to a boil, turn down and simmer 10 min.
Stir in hot roux and remove from heat.
Cool overnight.
Before reheating, add white wine and sour cream.

Potato - Cucumber Soup
- Yield 3 gals. -

3 onions diced
4 qts. water
10 lbs. potatoes peeled and sliced
1 cup chicken soup base
3 Tbl. dill weed
1 tsp. pepper
10 - 12 cucumbers peeled, seeded & cubed
4 cups sour cream

Brown onions in some butter.
Add water and bring to a boil.
Add potatoes, seasonings and cucumbers.
Bring back to a boil. Turn down and simmer until potatoes are just cooked (about 5 min.).
Refrigerate overnight.
Before re-heating stir in sour cream.

Gazpacho with Croutons
- yield 2 gals. -

2 #10 (102 oz) cans diced tomatoes
1 1/2 cups tomato paste
2 qts. water
1/2 cup olive oil
4 Tbl. sugar
4 Tbl. sweet basil
2 Tbl. dill weed
1/2 tsp. granulated garlic
4 Tbl. beef soup base diluted in ½ c. hot water
1 bunch parsley
2 green peppers
1 bunch celery
3-4 cucumbers peeled & seeded
1 bunch green onions
juice from 1 lemon
1 tsp. tabasco
1 Tbl. worcestershire sauce
salt & pepper to taste

Run tomatoes and vegetables through the food processor and chop coarsely.
Combine with all the rest of the ingredients and chill overnight.
Serve cold with croutons.

CROUTONS
6 qts. cubed stale bread
1 lb. butter
1 Tbl. dill weed
1/2 tsp. granulated garlic

Melt butter with dill and garlic. Pour over bread cubes and toss and fry until golden brown.

Cream Of Cauliflower Soup
- yield 4 gals. -

2 onions diced
2 lbs. carrots sliced
1 bunch celery sliced
6 qts. water
1 c. chicken soup base
1 tsp. bouquet garni
2 bay leaves
1 tsp. pepper
6 heads cauliflower cut bite sized
2 Tbl. lemon juice
1 qt. heavy cream <u>hot</u> (heat 12 min. in microwave)
1 bunch parsley, chopped
roux = 3 cups butter & 3 cups flour

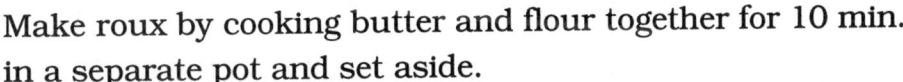

Make roux by cooking butter and flour together for 10 min. in a separate pot and set aside.
Sauté onions in some butter. Add carrots and celery and cook about 15 min. or until vegetables are fragrant. Add water, soup base and seasonings. Bring to a boil, add cauliflower and lemon juice. Bring back to a boil and cook 3-4 min. Then stir in <u>hot</u> roux and <u>hot</u> cream. Cook & stir until thick and remove from heat. Add chopped parsley.

14 Carrot Gold Soup
- yield 3 ½ gals. -

10 lbs. carrots scrubbed
7 qts. water
1 qt. orange juice
grated rind of 1 lg. orange
2 tsp. ground ginger
3 Tbl. granulated onion
2 Tbl. brown sugar
1 c. chicken soup base
roux = 2 c. butter & 2 c. flour

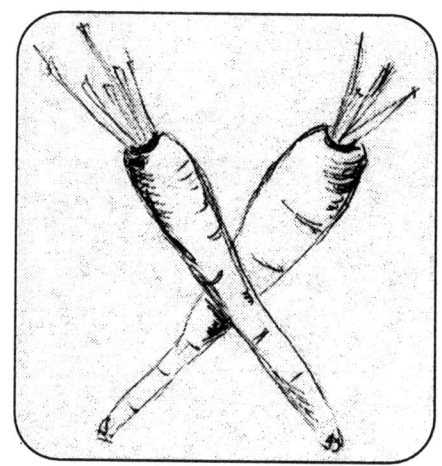

Make roux by cooking butter and flour together for 10 min. in a separate pot and set aside.

Bring 7 qts. water to a boil.

Slice 7 lbs. of the carrots and process 3 lbs. in the food processor until fine. Add to boiling water.

Then add orange rind and rest of the ingredients.

Bring back to a boil, turn down and simmer until carrot slices are tender (about 8 min.).

Last, whisk in <u>hot</u> roux and simmer until thickened.

Cuban Black Bean Soup
- yield 3 gals. -

soak 4-5 lbs. black turtle beans overnight
drain and add:
2 gals. water
1 tsp. granulated garlic
3 bay leaves
1 c. blackstrap molasses
1/4 tsp. cayenne pepper
1 tsp. tabasco
1 tsp. bouquet garni
1/2 c. ham soup base
1/2 c. beef soup base

1 lb. carrots
1 bunch celery → chop in food processor
3 green peppers
3 onions
2 1/2 lbs. cubed ham
roux = 1 c. bacon fat & 1 c. flour
4 c. cooked white rice

Make roux by cooking bacon fat and flour together for 5 min. & set aside. Bring beans and water to a boil. Turn down and add seasonings and molasses. Simmer 1 hour, then add processed vegetables and cubed ham. Return to a boil, turn down and simmer another 20 min. or until beans are cooked. Stir in <u>hot</u> roux. Add rice just before serving.

Boston Clam Chowder
- yield 4 gals. -

1 c. crumbled bacon
2-3 Tbl. bacon fat
6 onions diced
2 - 51 oz. cans chopped <u>sea</u> clams
1 46 oz. can <u>sea</u> clam juice
5 lbs. diced potatoes
salt to taste
2 tsp. pepper
1 tsp. bouquet garni
1 Tbl. dill weed
2 tsp. granulated garlic
1/4 tsp. cayenne pepper
6 qts. <u>hot</u> milk
roux = 3 c. butter & 3 c. flour
1 bunch parsley

Make roux by cooking butter and flour together for 10 min. and set aside.

Sauté onions in bacon fat. Add clams & juice and bring to a boil. Add potatoes and seasonings and cook until potatoes are barely done. Add <u>hot</u> milk and stir in <u>hot</u> roux. Cook until thickened and remove from heat.

Last add chopped parsley and crumbled bacon.

Ham and Dumpling Soup
- yield 4 gals. -

4 onions diced
2 lbs. carrots sliced
1 bunch celery sliced
2 gals. water
1 c. chicken soup base
1 tsp. pepper
1 Tbl. dill weed
3 Tbl. vinegar
2 1/2-3 lbs. cabbage cubed
2 1/2 lbs. diced ham

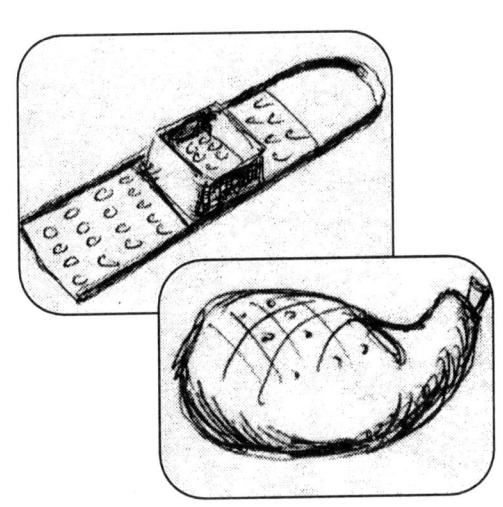

Dumplings:

| 6 eggs |
| 2 c. flour | → stir together with a fork
| 1 tsp. salt |

Brown onions, then add carrots & celery and sauté 15 min stirring often. Add water and seasonings. Bring to a boil and cook 10 min. Make dumplings right into boiling soup by plopping in teaspoons-full of batter, or use dumpling-maker pictured above.
Last add ham & cabbage, bring back to a boil and simmer 5 min. Garnish with parsley.

Lentil Vegetable Soup
- yield 3 1/2 gals. -

2 onions diced
2 lbs. carrots sliced
1 bunch celery sliced
1 green pepper diced
3 bay leaves
1 tsp. granulated garlic
1 tsp. pepper
3 Tbl. sugar
1/2 tsp. ground cloves
1 cup ham soup base
6 qts. water
1 #10 (102 oz.) can diced tomatoes
2 c. tomato paste
1/2 c. red wine vinegar
2 lbs. brown **or** red lentils

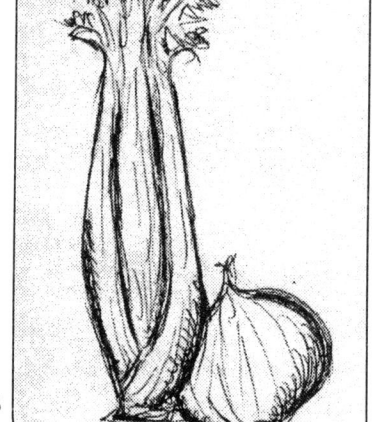

Brown onions.
Add carrots, celery and pepper.
Sauté about 20 min. stirring often.
Next add all the rest of the ingredients and bring to a boil.
Turn down and simmer 20-25 min. or until lentils are tender.
Remove from heat.

Garden Pea Soup
- yield 3 gals. -

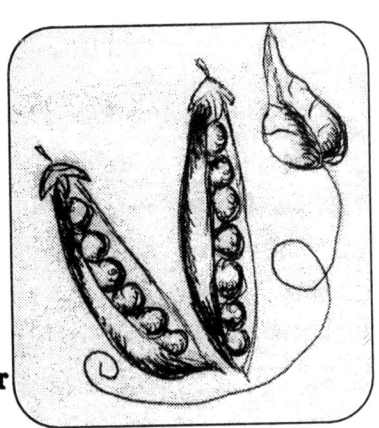

3 Tbl. butter
2 onions diced
10 lbs. frozen peas - thawed
1/2 c. fresh mint leaves chopped
4 Tbl. sugar
1 cup chicken soup base
2 gals. water
roux = 1 1/2 c. butter & 1 1/2 c. flour

Make roux by cooking butter and flour together 10 min. and set aside.
Lightly sauté onions in butter.
Add peas and mint; cook until peas are tender, 15-20 min.
Set aside 1/4 of the mixture and run the rest through the food processor.
Next put 2 gals. water in a large pot.
Add chicken base and sugar and bring to a boil.
Turn down and whisk in <u>hot</u> roux.
Then add pureéd pea mixture and the set aside whole peas.
Remove from heat and taste.

Cream of Potato Soup
- yield 3 gals. -

2 Tbl. butter
4 onions diced
10 lbs. potatoes peeled & sliced
1 tsp. pepper
1 bunch parsley & stems
1 c. chicken soup base
6 qts. water
1 qt. heavy cream <u>hot</u>
roux = 2 c. butter & 2 c. flour

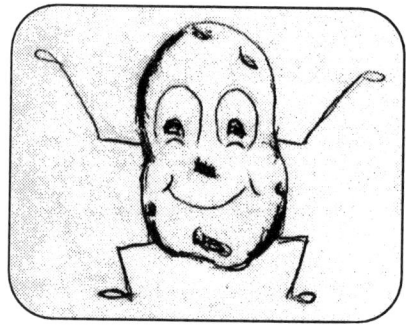

Make roux by cooking butter and flour together for 10 min. and set aside.

Lightly brown onions in butter.

Add water and bring to a boil.

Add seasonings, potatoes and just chopped <u>stems</u> of parsley. Bring back to a boil and cook about 5 min. or until potatoes are barely tender.

Heat heavy cream in microwave for 12 min. and add to soup.

Stir in <u>hot</u> roux until thickened.

Remove from heat and add chopped parsley.

Cream of Reuben Soup
- yield 3 gals. -

3 Tbl. butter
1 - 28 oz. can sauerkraut
4 onions diced
4 qts. water
1 c. chicken soup base
2 Tbl. Poupon mustard
1 tsp. horseradish
1 Tbl. dill weed
1 tsp. pepper
1 Tbl. sugar
8 c. cooked diced corned beef
8 c. shredded swiss cheese
6 qts. hot milk
roux = 3 c. butter & 3 c. flour

Make roux by cooking butter and flour together 10 min. and set aside.
Brown onions in butter.
Add sauerkraut and sauté 5-8 min.
Add water, soup base, seasonings and corned beef and bring to a boil. Turn down and simmer 5-6 min. Add <u>hot</u> milk, shredded swiss and <u>hot</u> roux stirring vigorously until soup is thick and smooth. Remove from heat.

Cream of Spinach Soup
- yield 3 gals. -

6 - 10 oz. pkgs. frozen chopped spinach, thawed
2 Tbl. butter
4 onions diced
3/4 c. chicken soup base
7 qts. water
1/2 tsp. nutmeg
1 qt. heavy cream <u>hot</u>
roux = 3 c. butter & 3 c. flour

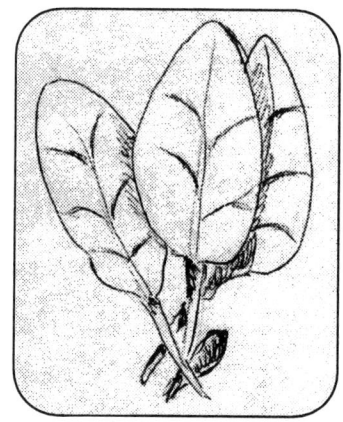

Make roux by cooking butter and flour together for 10 min. Set aside.
Lightly brown onions.
Add thawed spinach and cook 15-20 min.
Put mixture through food processor until very fine.
Return mixture to soup pot and add water, soup base and nutmeg.
Bring to a boil, turn down and whisk in <u>hot</u> roux.
Last stir in hot (12 min. in microwave) cream and remove from heat.

Tomato Dill Soup
- yield 4 gals. -

2 Tbl. butter
4 onions diced
2 qts. water
2 46 oz. cans tomato juice
2 #10 (102 oz.) cans diced tomatoes
4 1/2 c. tomato paste
2 1/2 c, honey
1/2 tsp. tabasco
3 tsp. granulated garlic
1 c. beef soup base
1 tsp. pepper
1/2 tsp. cayenne pepper
2 Tbl. chili powder
2 Tbl. sweet basil
3 Tbl. dill weed

Brown onions in butter.
Put diced tomatoes through food processor briefly so they are a little smaller. Add all ingredients to the pot and bring carefully to a boil stirring often. This soup likes to stick and burn! Simmer 15 min. and remove from heat.
Garnish with a dollop of sour cream and chopped parsley.

Cream of Turkey & Wild Rice Soup
- yield 3 1/2 gals.-

3 Tbl. butter
2 onions diced
1 bunch celery sliced
8 qts. water
3/4 c. turkey soup base
1/4 c. chicken soup base
1 tsp. bouquet garni
1 tsp. pepper
1 qt. heavy cream - <u>hot</u>
2 1/2 - 3 lbs. cubed cooked turkey
roux = 3 c. butter & 3 c. flour
2 qts. cooked wild rice blend

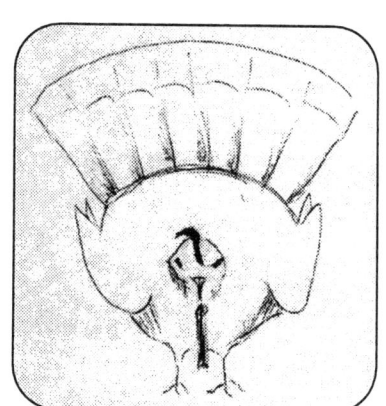

Make roux by cooking butter & flour together 10 min. Set aside.
Brown onions in butter.
Add celery and sauté about 6 min.
Add water and seasonings and bring to a boil.
Add turkey and return to a boil.
Turn down and stir in <u>hot</u> roux. Then stir in <u>hot</u> cream.
Continue cooking until thickened and remove from heat.
Just before serving, heat rice in microwave and add.

Cajun Bean Soup

-yield 4 gals. -

5 lbs. mixed or "calico" beans
6 qts. water
3/4 c. beef soup base
1/3 c. ham soup base
3 bay leaves
1 tsp. granulated garlic
3 Tbl. ground cumin
1/2 tsp. cayenne pepper
1 tsp. black pepper
1 tsp. tabasco
1/2 c. blackstrap molasses
1/2 c. honey
1 #10 (102 oz.) diced tomatoes

| 1 lb. carrots |
| 1 bunch celery |
| 3 onions |
| 3 green peppers |
| 3 Kielbasa sausages |

→ put all vegetables and Kielbasa through the food processor

Soak beans overnight. Drain and rinse.
Put beans, water, seasonings, honey & molasses in 5 gallon pot and bring to a boil.
Turn down and simmer 1 hour stirring occasionally.
Add processed veggies and kielbasa and return to a boil.
Simmer 15 min. or until beans are done.
Remove from heat.

Italian Barley Soup
-Yield 3 gals. -

3 Tbl. olive oil
3 onions diced
2 lbs. carrots sliced
1 bunch celery sliced
2 green peppers diced
6 qts. water
1 - 11 oz. box quick cooking barley
1 c. beef soup base
1/2 c. sweet basil
3 Tbl. oregano
1 tsp. granulated garlic
1 tsp. pepper
1 Tbl. sugar
2 c. tomato paste
1 #10 (102 oz.) can diced tomatoes
1/4 c. red wine vinegar

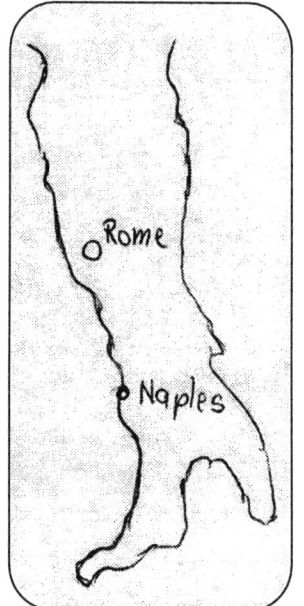

Brown onions in olive oil. Add carrots, celery, green peppers and sauté 20 min. stirring often. Next add all the rest of the ingredients and bring to a boil. Turn down and simmer 15 min. or until carrots are tender.
Before serving add **2 c. Burgundy wine.**
Garnish with grated parmesan cheese.

Chicken or Turkey & Dumpling Soup
- Yield 3 gals. -

2 Tbl. butter
2 onions diced
2 lbs. carrots sliced
2 bunches celery sliced
1 green pepper diced
6 qts. water
1 c. chicken soup base
(1 tsp. cajun magic opt.)
1 tsp. pepper
2 1/2 - 3 lbs. cooked cubed turkey or chicken
1 bunch parsley

Lightly brown onions. Add carrots, celery and green pepper and cook 15-20 min. Add water and seasonings. Bring to a boil and make dumplings right into the soup by plopping in teaspoons-full of batter, or use dumpling maker, pg 9.
Add turkey or chicken and bring back to a boil.
Remove from heat and add chopped parsley.

Dumplings:

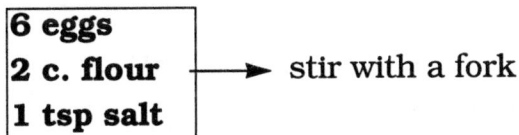

| 6 eggs |
| 2 c. flour | ⟶ stir with a fork
| 1 tsp salt |

Russian Borscht
- yield 3 gals. -

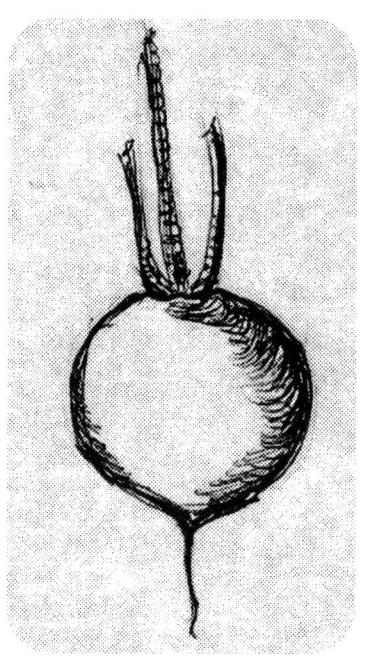

2 Tbl. butter
3 onions, diced
1 lb. carrots, sliced
1 bunch celery, sliced
6 qts. water
1 c. beef soup base
3 Tbl. dill weed
1 tsp. granulated garlic
1 tsp. pepper
1/4 c. red wine vinegar
2 Tbl. sugar
4 - 16 oz. cans sliced beets
3 lbs. cabbage cubed

Brown onions in butter. Add carrots & celery and sauté 10-15 min. until fragrant. Add water and seasonings and bring to a boil. Turn down and simmer until carrots are barely tender. (Drain beets and reserve juice. Slice beets into thin strips.)

Next add cabbage to the soup and bring back to a boil. Turn down and simmer 5 min.

Last, add beets and juice and remove from heat. Serve with a dollop of sour cream and a sprinkle of parsley.

Entrees and Other Stuff

Chicken Normandy
- yield 24 servings -

24 - 6oz. skinless, boneless chicken breasts
1 - 13 oz. pkg. rice krispies
4 eggs
1/2 c. milk
1 lb. melted butter
dusting of pepper

Run rice krispies through the blender until they are very fine, like flour.
Mix together eggs and milk. Dip chicken in egg-milk mixture then in rice krispy flour. Place on foil covered pans. Paint liberally with melted butter, and dust with pepper.
Bake in hot oven 425 - 450° for 20 min. Rotate pans and bake another 10 min. or until nice and brown.
Remove from oven and top with
Sauce Normandy:
1 - 50 oz. can cream of mushroom soup
3 c. heavy cream
Mix and heat.

Serve over wild rice blend.
1 36 oz. pkg. wild rice blend

Alaska Crab Sandwich
- yield 30 servings -

3 lbs. cream cheese, softened
5 lbs. shredded crab, plus legs
1 1/2 c. mayonnaise
3 Tbl. granulated onion
3 Tbl. dill weed
3 Tbl. chopped parsley
3 Tbl. lemon juice
2 tsp. horseradish
1/2 tsp. bouquet garni
1 Tbl. sugar
1/2 tsp. tabasco
1 tsp. **beaumond** (opt.)
2 c. fresh bread crumbs
2-3 c. toasted almonds for garnish

Put cream cheese in mixer and beat 2 min.
Add mayonnaise and seasonings, blending well.
Stir in bread crumbs and shredded crab by hand.
Put mixture in a covered pan and bake at 350° 1 hour or until hot throughout.
Heat crab legs separately in a covered pan for 20 min.
To serve:
Grill a slice of bread until golden on one side. Spread crab mixture over untoasted side. Top with hot crab legs and toasted almonds.

Creôle Shrimp with Rice
- yield 1- 1/2 gal. -

6 lbs. cooked shrimp
1 c. butter
8 c. onions diced
3 c. green peppers diced
2 c. celery sliced
1/2 c. flour
2 tsp. thyme
3 bay leaves
1/2 tsp. cayenne pepper
1 tsp. black pepper
1 Tbl. salt
2 Tbl. worcestershire
2 tsp. tabasco
2 c. dry vermouth
2 cans (1 lb. 12 oz.) diced tomatoes

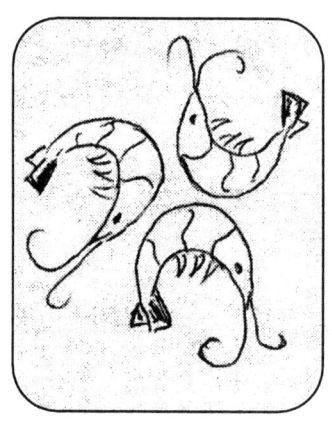

Brown onions in butter.
Add green peppers and celery and sauté until tender.
Stir in flour and cook 5 min.
Then add everything except shrimp.
Stir and cook until mixture comes to a boil.
Turn down, add shrimp and cook until shrimp are hot.
Remove from heat and serve over rice.

Ratatouille
- yield 5 qts. -

2 lbs. eggplant cubed
2 lbs. zucchini sliced
2 lbs. onions 1"dice
4 green peppers 1" dice
4 red peppers 1"dice
8 cloves garlic minced
4 lbs. canned whole tomatoes
12 oz. olive oil
1 c. chopped parsley
2 bay leaves
1/2 tsp. thyme
salt & pepper to taste
roux = 1/2 c. butter & 1/2 c. flour

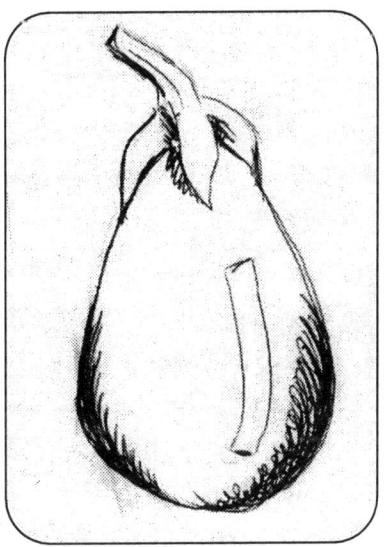

Make roux by cooking butter & flour together 5 min. & set aside. Sauté veggies separately in olive oil.
As you finish with each kind, put it in a large pot.
Add tomatoes and seasonings.
Bring to a boil stirring often.
Turn down and simmer 10 min.
Add roux and stir until thickened. Remove from heat.
To use for an omelette; put ratatouille inside and sprinkle with parmesan cheese.
Fold omelette out onto a plate and top with mozzarella.

Stroganoff
- yield 3 gals. -

10 lbs. ground chuck
1 gal. onions diced
1 c. flour
6 Tbl. sweet basil
2 Tbl. dill weed
5 Tbl. beef soup base (diluted in 1/2 c. hot water)
2 tsp. pepper
2 tsp. granulated garlic
2 Tbl. worcestershire
2 c. white wine (Chablis)
1 c. tomato paste
4 lbs. button mushrooms sliced
1 qt. sour cream

Brown onions and set aside. Sauté mushrooms and set aside. Brown ground beef and stir in 1 c. flour.
Add the rest of the dry ingredients. Stir in beef soup base, tomato paste, worcestershire and white wine.
Add cooked onions and mushrooms and bring up to heat. Last add sour cream.
Serve over wild rice blend and top with a dollop of sour cream and a sprinkle of paprika.

Verna's Sandwich
- yield 15 servings -

1 1/2 lbs. cream cheese softened
48 oz. canned albacore - drained
3/4 c. mayonnaise
2 Tbl. granulated onion
2 Tbl. dill weed
3 Tbl. chopped parsley
1 Tbl. lemon juice
1 tsp. horseradish
1/2 tsp. bouquet garni
1 tsp. sugar
1 tsp. tabasco
1 tsp. beaumond
1 c. soft bread crumbs
3 c. seeded & diced tomatoes

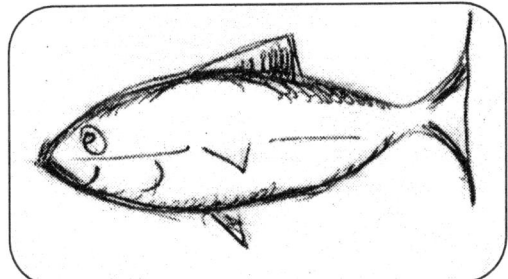

Place cream cheese in mixer and beat 2-3 min.
Add mayonnaise and seasonings, blending well.
Stir in albacore and bread crumbs by hand.
Bake covered at 350° for 1 hr.

To serve:
Grill a slice of bread on one side. Spread mixture on ungrilled side. Top with diced tomatoes and parsley.

New Orleans' Red Beans & Rice
- yield - 7 qts. -

4 onions diced
4 green peppers diced
1 bunch celery sliced
1 #10 (102 oz.) can small red beans
3 Kielbasa sliced
1 c. salsa
2 Tbl. tomato paste
cajun seasoning*
1 c. roux = 1/2 c. butter & 1/2 c. flour
cooked white rice

*Cajun Seasoning:

1 Tbl. ham soup base	1 tsp. cayenne pepper
1 Tbl. beef soup base	1 tsp. thyme
1 Tbl. paprika	2 tsp. basil
1 tsp. black pepper	2 Tbl. granulated onion
	1 tsp. granulated garlic

Make roux by cooking butter & flour together for 10 min. stirring occasionally. Set aside.

Brown onions. Add green peppers & celery and brown them too. In a separate pan brown Kielbasa and set aside.
To the vegetables add beans, salsa, tomato paste, cajun seasoning and browned Kielbasa.
Bring to a boil, stir in roux, turn down & simmer 20 min. stirring often. Serve over white rice.
Can also be served in a omelette or turned into soup.

Tørsk
- yield 10 servings -

5 lbs. Icelandic cod filets
6-7 lbs. new red potatoes
2 gals. court bouillon
melted butter & chopped parsley

Court Bouillon:
2 gals. water
1 c. lemon juice concentrate
1 c. red wine vinegar
1 onion sliced
1 lemon sliced
1/2 c. salt
1 tsp. peppercorns
2 bay leaves
1 bunch parsley **stems**
1/2 tsp. thyme

> Combine all ingredients on the left, and bring to a boil. Then turn down and simmer 1/2 hr. Strain through a towel. Can be made the day before.

Thaw fish in the refrigerator overnight.
Cut into 8 oz. pieces. Bring court bouillon to a boil. Plunge fish in and turn heat down to low. Cover and poach fish about 12 min.
Serve with boiled potatoes, melted butter and chopped parsley.
You may keep & re- use court bouillon for a couple of days.

Tamale Torte
- yield 4 - 9x13 pans -

Meat mixture:
10 lbs. ground beef
1 #10 (102 oz.) can diced tomatoes
4 onions diced
6- 1 1/4 oz. pkgs. taco seasoning

Wet Mix:
14 eggs
5 c. sour cream
3 lbs. thawed corn
1 28 oz. can chopped green chilies
2 lbs. shredded cheese
1 c. salsa

Dry Mix:
12 c. cornmeal
3 Tbl. baking powder
1 Tbl. baking soda
1/4 c. sugar
1 Tbl. salt

Brown onions and set aside.
Brown hamburger and drain off excess fat.
Add taco seasoning, tomatoes and browned onions.
Simmer 5-8 min. and remove from heat.
Make wet mix by whisking eggs, then stir in all the rest of the wet ingredients.
Mix dry ingredients together. Add wet mix to dry mix and fold in quickly. Divide 2/3 of the batter between 4- 9x13 pans. Divide meat mixture equally, spooning it carefully over the batter. Dot with remaining 1/3 of the batter.
Bake at 350° for 1 1/4 hrs. Rotate pans after 45 min.
To serve top with chopped black olives and sour cream.

Warm Chicken Salad with Orange/Rosemary Dressing
- yield 24 servings -

24 - 6 oz. chicken breasts trimmed and flattened
Seasoned salt
3 c. craisins (dried cranberries)
24 white bread ends or slices
salad greens and vegetables

Grill chicken with seasoned salt about 5 min. on each side.
Slice across the grain and lay on salad greens.
Top with some craisins and warm orange rosemary dressing.
Garnish with black olives, orange slices and a slice of
garlic toast.

Orange Rosemary Dressing: - yield 6 cups -

2 onions diced & browned in
1/2 c. butter.
Add 1/2 c. flour & cook 5 min.

3 Tbl. grated orange rind
1 Tbl. ground rosemary
1 Tbl. salt

Then add the following:
4 c. orange juice
1 c. red wine vinegar
1/2 c. cranberry juice
1/3 c. sugar

1 tsp. pepper
1 tsp. granulated garlic
*1 1/2 c. salad oil (added last - see below)

Bring to a boil, turn down and simmer 3 min.
Last, whisk in salad oil and serve warm with Garlic Toast as
described on the next page.

Garlic Toast: - yield 24 -

Seasoned butter:

Melt:

1 lb. butter
1 Tbl. dill weed
1/2 tsp. granulated garlic

Brush bread with the above and place on cookie sheets. Bake at 450° for 10 min. Turn pans and continue baking until brown and crispy.

Honey Mustard Dressing
- yield 6 cups -

1/2 c. butter
2 onions diced
1/2 c. flour
4 c. orange juice
1 c. red wine vinegar
1 c. honey
1/2 c. country dijon mustard
1 Tbl. salt
1 tsp. pepper
1 tsp. granulated garlic
1 Tbl. dill weed
1 1/2 c. corn oil - added last

Brown onions in butter. Add flour and cook 5 min.
Next add liquids and seasonings.
Bring to a boil, turn down and simmer 5 min.
Last whisk in corn oil and remove from heat.
Serve as a warm salad dressing.

Beulah's Salad Dressing
- yield 1 gal. -

1 c. country dijon mustard
3 bunches parsley (or 3 c. chopped packed)
1/4 c. granulated onion
1 c. concentrated lemon juice
3 c. red wine vinegar
2 c. sugar
1/2 c. salt
2 Tbl. pepper
1 tsp. granulated garlic
1 Tbl. worcestershire
1 Tbl. dill weed
8 c. corn oil

Run all the ingredients through the blender in batches, and combine in a gallon container.

Sauce Moreau
- yield 7 cups -

Roux = 1/4 c. butter & 1/4 c. flour
6 c. heavy cream
1/2 c. Grey Poupon mustard
1/2 tsp. pepper

Make brown roux by cooking butter and flour together until a dark nutty brown. Heat cream and add seasonings. Whisk in roux, stirring until thickened.

Oma's Bread Stuffing
- yield 2 - 9x13 pans -

2 gals. cubed stale bread
1/4 lb. butter
3 onions diced
3 stalks celery sliced
3 eggs
3 c. chicken stock
3 tsp. sugar
3 tsp. poultry seasoning
1 tsp. ground rosemary
1 tsp. pepper

Lightly brown onions in butter.
Add celery and sauté until tender.
Put bread cubes in a large bowl and pour everything else on top, including onions and celery.
Toss gently with hands until combined.
Spread in 2 - 9x13 pans and bake in a 350° oven for 45-60 min.

Cakes and Pies

Cranberry Nut Pie
- yield 1 - 9" pie -

1- unbaked 9" pie shell
1 1/2 sticks butter
2 c. cranberries
1/2 c. brown sugar
1/2 c. walnuts
2 eggs
3/4 c. white sugar
3/4 c. flour

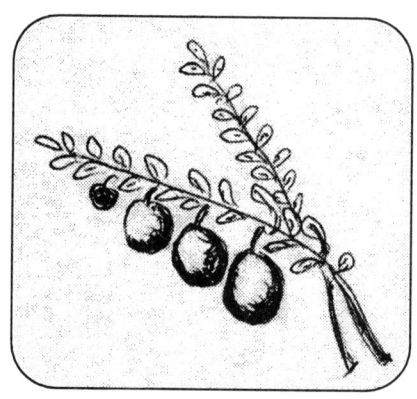

Melt butter and set aside to cool.
Layer cranberries, brown sugar and walnuts in the pie shell.
In the mixer, beat eggs with a whisk 4-5 min. at maximum speed.
Add white sugar and continue beating on high until light and thick.
Add cooled butter <u>slowly</u>, continuing to whip.
Last fold in flour with a spatula.
Pile mixture on top of cranberries and smooth out to the edges of the pie shell.
Bake at 350° 45-50 min. or until brown and set in the middle.

Granny Smith Apple Pie
- yield 2 - 9" pies -

2 unbaked 9" pie shells
10 c. peeled sliced apples
1/2 c. butter/margarine
1 1/4 c. water
2 tsp. vanilla
1 1/2 c. sugar
1 tsp. cinnamon
6 Tbl. flour
1/4 tsp. salt
1/2 tsp. nutmeg

Cook apples, butter, water & vanilla in a covered pot until apples are barely tender.
Mix together dry ingredients and stir into apples. Keep cooking and stirring until mixture thickens.
Remove from heat. Pour equally into pie shells and top with

Streusel:
2 c. flour
2 sticks cold butter (1 c.)
1/2 c. sugar

Put everything in the food processor and run until mixture is very lumpy.
Sprinkle evenly over apples. Bake at 425° for 30-35 min. or until bubbly and golden brown.

Banana Cake
- yield 1- 9x13 pan -

1 1/2 c. butter/margarine mix
1 1/2 c. sugar
3 eggs
1 1/2 c. mashed bananas
2 1/2 c. flour
1 1/2 tsp. baking powder
1/2 tsp. salt
1 tsp. vanilla

Cream butter & sugar. Beat in eggs, bananas and vanilla.
Sift dry ingredients together and add.
Spread in buttered 9 x13 pan and add

Topping:
1 c. coarsely chopped walnuts
1 c. coconut
1 c. brown sugar
1/4 lb. cold butter

Put all dry ingredients in a bowl. Slice in hard butter.
Work everything with fingers until blended and lumpy.
Sprinkle over cake batter.
Bake at 350° for 45 min. or until it tests done.
Cool and drizzle with thin powdered sugar icing.

Cheesecake
- yield 1 - 9" cake -

Crust:
1 c. flour
1/4 lb. cold butter
2 Tbl. sugar

Filling:
1 1/2 lb. cream cheese
1 c. cottage cheese
1 c. sour cream
4 eggs
1 1/2 c. sugar
2 Tbl. lemon juice
1 tsp. vanilla
3 Tbl. cornstarch

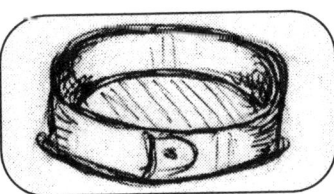

Topping:
2 c. sour cream
3 Tbl. sugar
1/2 tsp. vanilla

Put crust ingredients into a food processor and run until lumpy. Press crust into a 9" springform pan, covering bottom & halfway up the sides.
Bake at 350° 15-18 min, or until slightly brown.
Put all filling ingredients into food processor and run until smooth and creamy.
Put filling into baked crust and bake at 350° 1 hr. 10 min.
Mix topping, and cover top of cheesecake.
Return to oven and bake for 10 min.
Cool, then chill overnight before serving to achieve the best texture and flavor.

Carrot Cake
- yield 1 cake -

4 eggs
1 1/4 c. salad oil
2 c. sugar
1 tsp. vanilla
1/2 tsp. coconut extract
2 c. flour
1 tsp. baking powder
1 tsp. baking soda
1 tsp. salt
1 tsp. nutmeg
1 tsp. cinnamon
2 c. grated carrots
3/4 c. raisins
3/4 c. walnuts

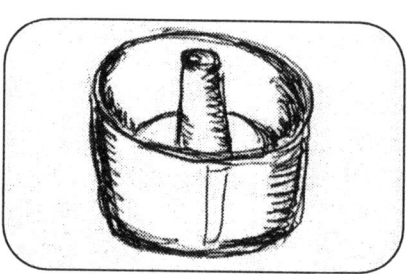

Frosting:
4 oz. cream cheese
1/4 c. butter/margarine
3 c. powdered sugar
1/2 tsp. vanilla

Beat eggs until light and fluffy.
Add sugar and oil while beating on high.
Add vanilla and coconut extract.
Mix dry ingredients and stir in on low speed.
Add carrots, raisins & nuts.
Pour into a buttered tube pan and bake at 350° for 1 hr. or until it tests done.
Cool and spread with cream cheese frosting

Coffee Cakes
- yield 3 - 8" square cakes -

2 c. butter/margarine
3 c. sugar
9 eggs
6 c. flour
1 Tbl. baking powder
1 Tbl. baking soda
1 1/2 tsp. salt
1 Tbl. vanilla
1 lemon - juice of
3 c. sour cream

<u>Topping:</u>
mix together:
1 1/2 c. brown sugar
1 1/2 tsp. cinnamon
1 1/2 c. old fashioned oatmeal

2 c. chopped walnuts

Cream butter & sugar.
Add eggs one at a time.
Add lemon juice & vanilla.
Sift dry ingredients together and add alternately with sour cream.
Divide batter into 3 buttered & floured 8" pans and sprinkle with topping and walnuts.
Bake at 360° for 45 min.

Custard Cups
- yield 7 - 5 oz. cups -

**5 eggs
1/2 c. sugar
1/4 tsp. salt
1 3/4 c. milk
3/4 c. heavy cream
1 tsp. vanilla
nutmeg, a sprinkle**

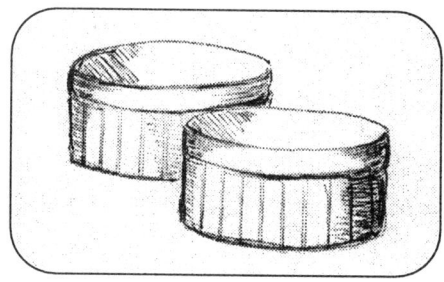

Stir eggs until well blended.
Add everything except nutmeg and stir well.
Place 7 empty custard cups in a 9x13 pan with 2 c. water.
Fill custard cups, sprinkle with nutmeg and bake at 350° for 45-50 min. or until barely set.
Remove from oven. Take cups out of baking pan.
Chill and serve.

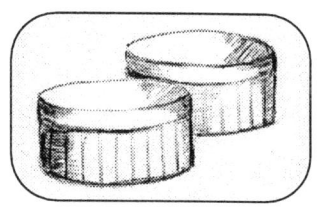

Cinnamon Rolls
- yield 30 - 5oz. rolls -

| 1 c. hot (110°-118°) water |
| 3 Tbl. dry yeast |
| 1 Tbl. sugar |

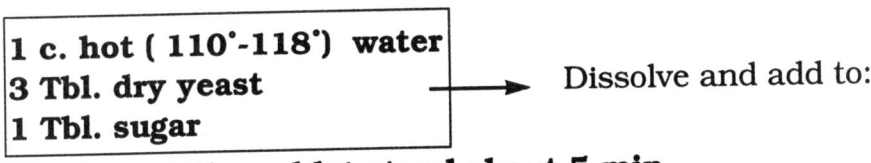 Dissolve and add to:

1 c. flour. Stir and let stand about 5 min.

Then add:
3 eggs
1 c. corn oil
1 tsp. vanilla
1 c. sugar
1 Tbl. salt
8 c. flour
3 1/2 c. hot (110°) water

| **Filling:** use 1/2 for each piece |
| 1 c. melted butter |
| 2 c. brown sugar |
| 1 c. raisins |
| 1 Tbl. cinnamon |
| walnuts & craisins opt. |

Stir everything together.
Put dough hook on mixer and beat on med. speed 3-4 min.
Remove dough to well floured surface and knead a few min.
Place in oiled bowl to rise for 20-30 min.
Divide dough in half. Roll into a 30" by 20" rectangle.
Spread with 1/2 the filling and roll up firmly.
Cut into 15 pieces. Place cut side down on sheet pans and flatten slightly.
Let rise 30 min. then bake at 360° for 20 min.
Rotate pans and bake 10 min. more.
While still warm paint with powdered sugar icing.

Meggie's Crunchy Granola
- yield 1 1/2 gals. -

1 - 42 oz. box old fashioned oatmeal
2 c. wheat germ
1 1/2 c. brown sugar
4 c. raw sunflower seeds
4 c. sliced almonds
1 Tbl. salt
1 1/2 c. corn oil
2/3 c. water
1 c. honey
1 Tbl. vanilla

Mix dry ingredients together.
Mix wet ingredients together.
Combine wet & dry and mix well.
Spread 1/2" thick on 3 or 4 sheet pans.
Bake a 360° for 20 min. Rotate pans and bake 10 min. more.
Stir granola and return to oven for another 5-10 min.
Continue to stir and bake until a dark toasty brown.
Remove from oven and stir in:

2 c. raisins
2 c. craisins (dry cranberries)

Cool and store in air tight containers.

Poppy Seed Torte

- yield 2 - 8" layers -

Soak for 1 hour:
1 c. milk
1/3 cup poppy seeds

Cream:
1 c. butter/margerine
1 1/2 c. sugar
Add 1 1/2 tsp. vanilla

Sift together:
1 3/4 c. flour
2 1/2 tsp. baking powder
1/4 tsp. salt

Add dry and wet ingredients alternately to creamed mixture.
Beat **6 egg whites** and fold into batter. Bake at 375° for 28 min. in 2 buttered, floured 8" pans. Cool 15 min. before removing from pans. When cool, split layers and fill.

Filling:
1/2 c. sugar
2 Tbl. cornstarch
1 3/4 c. milk
6 egg yolks
1 tsp. vanilla
pinch of salt

Combine and bring to a boil whisking constantly.
Remove from heat and whisk in 1 Tbl. butter/marg.
Spread filling on first layer and sprinkle with
1/3 c. chopped walnuts.
Fill the next two layers and top with a dusting of powdered sugar.

Pumpkin Pies
- yield 2- 9" pies

2 unbaked pie shells
6 eggs beaten
1 can pumpkin (*Libby's* 29 oz.) or 4 c.
1 c. brown sugar
1/2 c. blackstrap molasses
1/2 c. sugar
2 tsp. cinnamon
1 tsp. ground ginger
1/2 tsp. cloves
1 tsp. nutmeg
1 tsp. vanilla
1/4 tsp. salt
2 c. milk
1 c. heavy cream

Mix and pour into pie shells.
Bake 1 hour at 375° or until pie tests done.
Make a 3" slit in the middle after removing from the oven.
This way you can control the cracking that always seems to happen to pumpkin pies.

Pie Shells
- yield 2 -

2 c. flour
5 oz. vegetable shortening
1 tsp. salt
1 Tbl. sugar
1/2 c. ice water

Put flour, shortening, salt & sugar in food processor.
Run until crumbly. While still running, add cold water and keep going until dough forms a ball.
Remove and divide ball in half to make two patties.
Wrap in plastic and chill overnight.
Put in microwave 15 sec. to soften slightly before rolling out.

Pumpkin Cake
- yield 1- 9 x13 or 1 tube pan -

2 c. sugar
4 eggs
2 c. (*Libby's*) pumpkin
3/4 c. melted butter - cooled
1 tsp. ground ginger
1/4 tsp. cloves
2 c. flour
2 tsp. baking powder
1 tsp. baking soda
1/2 tsp. salt
1 tsp. cinnamon
1 tsp. nutmeg
1 tsp. vanilla
1 c. chopped walnuts
1 c. raisins

Beat eggs, then add sugar and continue beating until light. Add cooled melted butter slowly continuing to beat on high. Stir in pumpkin and vanilla. Fold in mixed dry ingredients, walnuts and raisins.

Pour into buttered floured tube or 9x13 pan. Bake at 350° - 50 min. or until cake tests done.

Frost with **Cream Cheese Frosting:**
4 oz. cream cheese
1/2 c. butter/marg.
3 c. powdered sugar
1/2 tsp. vanilla

Strawberry Torte
- yield 1 - 10" torte -

4 c. whole fresh strawberries
1/3 c. cold water
1/4 c. raspberry brandy
1/4 c. cornstarch
1 c. sugar
1 tsp. vanilla
1/2 tsp. red food color

Arrange 2 c. berries on sponge cake and heat the other 2 c. of berries in the microwave for 3 min. Put them in a saucepan and mash with a potato masher.
Stir water, brandy and cornstarch together. Add everything to mashed berries and bring to a boil stirring constantly. Boil 1 min. then pour over berries on sponge cake. Chill & serve with whipped cream.

Sponge Cake
3 eggs
1/2 c. sugar
1/2 c. flour
1/2 tsp. baking powder
1/4 tsp. salt
1/2 tsp. vanilla
1/2 tsp. lemon juice

Beat eggs 5 min. Add sugar and continue to beat until thick. Add lemon juice and vanilla.
Mix dry ingredients and fold in by hand. Pour into buttered, floured 10" flan pan and bake at 375° for 19-20 min. Remove from pan and cool.

Swedish Apple Pies
- yield 2 - 9" pies -

2 unbaked 9" pie shells
8 c. sliced granny smith apples
4 Tbl. flour
2 c. sour cream
2 beaten eggs
1 tsp. vanilla
1/4 tsp. salt
1 1/2 c. sugar
grated rind and juice of 1 lemon

Put sliced apples into 2 empty pie plates, cover with plastic-wrap & microwave 5 min. each.
Now put apples into unbaked pie shells.
Mix all other ingredients together and pour over pies.
Top with streusel.

Streusel:
2 c. flour
1/2 lb. cold butter sliced
1/2 c. sugar
1 tsp. cinnamon

Put everything in the food processor and run until lumpy. Sprinkle over pies.
Bake at 400° - 15 min. then reduce heat to 375° and bake 40 min. more.

Walnut Pie
- yield 1 - 9" pie -

1 unbaked 9" pie shell
4 eggs slightly beaten
1 c. brown sugar
1 c. light *Karo* syrup
1/4 tsp. maple extract
1/4 tsp. salt
1/4 c. melted butter
1 tsp. vanilla
1 1/2 c. walnut pieces

Mix everything together and pour into unbaked pie shell. Bake at 375° for 55-60 min. or until the pie has risen and the middle is set.

French Chocolate Torte

- yield 1 - 10" torte -

1 sponge cake - flan shaped (see pg. 49)
2 oz. bitter chocolate
1/2 c. butter/marg. mix
4 oz. cream cheese
1 c. sugar
2 egg yolks
1/8 tsp. rum extract
1 tsp. vanilla
 pinch salt
1/4 c. powdered sugar
1 c. heavy whipping cream
semi-sweet choc. for garnish

Melt chocolate and cool to room temp.
Cream butter, cream cheese & sugar.
Add egg yolks and beat well.
Add vanilla, rum extract and salt.
Now add melted chocolate and whip until smooth & creamy.
In a separate bowl beat whipping cream with powdered sugar until stiff.
Fold whipped cream into chocolate mixture.
Pile it all onto the sponge cake and spread it out.
Top with shaved semi-sweet chocolate or drizzle with melted chocolate. Chill & serve.

Chocolate Cake

- yield 2 - 8" layers -

3 oz. bitter chocolate
1/3 c. water
1 c. whipped butter/marg.
2 1/4 c. brown sugar
2 eggs
1 tsp. vanilla
1 c. water
2 c. flour
1 tsp. baking soda
1/2 tsp. salt

Melt chocolate in 1/3 c. water and cool to room temp.
Cream butter & sugar.
Add eggs & vanilla, beat well.
Add chocolate mixture.
Sift dry ingredients and add alternately with 1 cup water.
Pour into 2 buttered, floured 8" cake pans.
Bake at 350° for 30-35 min. or until cake tests done.
Cool 15 min. before removing from pans.
For a fancy cake, split the layers and fill with French Chocolate on page 52, and dust with powdered sugar.

Rhubarb Pie

- yield 2 - 9" pies -

2 unbaked pie shells
8 c. fresh rhubarb
4 Tbl. quick tapioca
2 Tbl. cornstarch
3 eggs, beaten
1/2 tsp. salt
2 c. brown sugar
1/2 tsp. nutmeg
2 tsp. vanilla

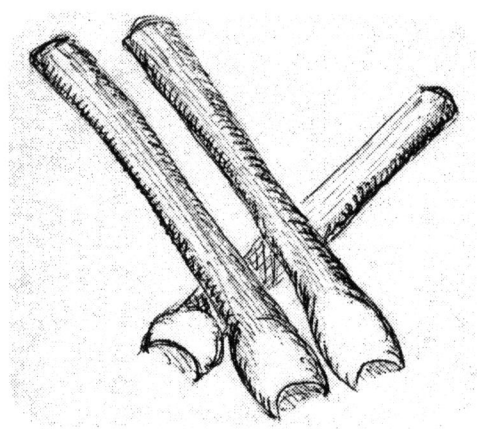

Cut rhubarb into 1" pieces and place in a bowl.
Add the rest of the ingredients and mix well.
Let the mixture sit 20-30 min. until it's soupy, then put it into the pie shells and top with streusel.

Streusel:
2 c. flour
2 sticks cold butter
1/2 c. sugar

Put everything into the food processor and run until lumpy.
Sprinkle over the pies.
Bake at 360° for 1 hour until brown and bubbly.

Index

Beautiful Soups

Barley, Italian, 18
Borscht, Russian, 20
Boston Clam Chowder, 8
Cajun Bean, 17
Chicken Dumpling, 19
Clam Chowder, Boston, 8
Cream of:
   Cauliflower, 5
   Potato, 12
   Spinach, 14
   Reuben, 13
Cuban Black Bean, 7
Fourteen, 14 Carrot Gold, 6
Croutons, 4
Garden Pea, 11
Gazpacho, 4
Ham & Dumpling, 9
Italian Barley, 18
Lentil, 10
Lou's Mushroom, 2
Mushroom, Lou's, 2
Pea, Garden, 11
Potato, Cream of, 12
Potato Cucumber, 3
Reuben, Cream of, 13
Roux, 2
Russian Borscht, 20
Spinach, Cream of, 14
Tomato Dill, 15
Turkey & Dumpling, 19
Turkey & Wild Rice, 16

Entrees & Other Stuff

Alaska Crab Sandwich, 23
Beulah's Salad Dressing, 33
Bread Stuffing, Oma's, 34
Chicken Normandy, 22
Chicken Salad, Warm, 31
Crab Sandwich, Alaska, 23
Créôle Shrimp with rice, 24
Croutons, 4
Garlic Toast, 32
Honey Mustard Dressing, 32
New orleans Red Beans & Rice, 28
Normandy, Chicken, 22
Orange Rosemary Dressing, 31
Ratatouille, 25
Red Beans & Rice, 28
Rosemary, Orange Dressing, 31
Salad, Warm Chicken, 31
Salad Dressing:
   Beulah's, 33
   Honey Mustard, 32
   Orange Rosemary, 31
Sauce Moreau, 33
Shrimp, Créôle, 24
Stroganoff, 26
Stuffing, Oma's, 34
Tamale Torte, 30
Tørsk, 29
Verna's Sandwich, 27
Warm Chicken Salad, 31

Pies & Cakes

Apple Pies, Granny Smith, 37
Banana Cake, 38
Cakes:
  Banana, 38
  Carrot, 40
  Cheesecake, 39
  Chocolate, 53
  Coffee, 41
  Pumpkin, 48
  Sponge, 49
Carrot Cake, 40
Cheesecake, 39
Chocolate Cake, 53
Chocolate, French Torte, 52
Cinnamon Rolls, 42
Coffee Cakes, 41
Crunchy Granola, Meggie's, 44
Custard Cups, 42
French Chocolate Torte, 52
Granola, Meggie's Crunchy, 44

Pies:
  Apple, Granny Smith, 37
  Apple, Swedish, 50
  Cranberry Nut, 36
  Rhubarb, 54
  Pumpkin, 46
  Walnut, 51
Pie Shells, 47
Poppy Seed Torte, 45
Pumpkin Cake, 48
Pumpkin Pie, 46
Rhubarb Pie, 54
Strawberry Torte, 49
Streusel, 37
Sponge Cake, 49
Swedish Apple Pie, 50
Tortes:
  French Chocolate, 52
  Poppy Seed, 45
  Strawberry, 49